GOOD BOYS

Copyright © 2020 Megan Fernandes

Published by Tin House Books, Portland, Oregon

Distributed by W. W. Norton & Company

Library of Congress Cataloging-in-Publication Data

Names: Fernandes, Megan, author.
Title: Good boys / Megan Fernandes.
Description: Portland, Oregon : Tin House Books, [2020]
Identifiers: LCCN 2019031495 | ISBN 9781947793408 (paperback) |
    ISBN 9781947793491 (ebook)
Classification: LCC PS3606.E7328 A6 2020 | DDC 811/.6—dc23
LC record available at https://lccn.loc.gov/2019031495

First U.S. Edition 2020
Printed in the USA
Interior design by Jakob Vala

www.tinhouse.com

GOOD BOYS

POEMS

MEGAN FERNANDES

 TIN HOUSE BOOKS / Portland, Oregon

For my sisters:
Micaela & Mia & Judith

CONTENTS

I

II

III

I

IN WHICH I BECOME A MYTHOLOGY AND ALSO, EXECUTED

Sometimes I could see my parents
spiraling in the Americas,

in the opera rooms and dives,
in the bodega where the VCR

played Bollywood in Northeast Philly
near where my dad worked.

In January, I will visit India
and fail there too, because

I am childless
or because I am in America

where they gun down
babies

or because
I took too long

to come back. Somedays
I close my eyes and imagine

a body of land
without relatives, like Iceland

and her flagrant
light, flaring in dance

with those magnetic poles—
a green current whistling

across my eyelids.
I always arrive a little broken

to those scenes,
bundled, like a seer

peering into a bucket
and I want to throw myself

in and come out
dainty, come out graceful.

Grace is a word that stings.
Because if you don't have it,

you are not a lady.

And if you are not a lady,
then what are you.

Chucked meat.
Beast girl on speed.

My parents hardly ever let me go
on sleepovers

to any girl's house
unless she was an immigrant.

I had a Greek friend.
And Chinese.

We had curfews and got slapped
hard for mouthing off.

We grew into dragons
and ate too many pills in college

groveling on a floor
that could barely pass

for a forest
like a centaur that has been shot

and pulled along
by rope—

the weight of the horse's body,
offending everyone.

INDIGO

We have called the goat Oona, and she is bleeding out a kid. The river like felt eels, graveyards like cities. My niece and I sit and watch Oona miscarry, the drop of soft head, her gaze transfixed on an astral plane, pleading. This is the countryside in France. These animals. Night bunnies. Pepped chickens with their snapping eggs. Oona is in the starlight among them. The thistle casts her face in blue, and Indigo asks: Does this happen to humans, too? Four streets, one called Rue du Midi, where I would push my niece in a stroller past a war memorial with eighteen names. Yes, it happens to humans, too. The kid is born on thistle spikes. Oona licks his face. When we walk home, Indigo is charging into black. I strain to hear her feet. I don't tell her about the phone call, how we held our breath across the Atlantic. She would be an Iris or an Indigo my sister told me. If she would be at all.

AMSTERDAM

Sometimes the mythologies of a city are true
like when I see a blond man bob for red apples
selling records side by side with a black cat wound
in a cushion, deep in dream. Josh says he does not want
to go see Anne Frank, that that kind of tourism
depresses him, the one where the demonstration of grief
is like a voyeuristic tug at suffering
that is not yours to possess. *How do you eat a meal after that.*
He seems sad today. *How do you stay alive.*
When he was young, he visited Auschwitz and told
me not to go because it had a gift shop and that
made him angry and nobody knows how to grieve
in public, how to make public space for loss
unless you can make money off of it but really
there is something else to his anger, the child
abandoned, the residue of a young girl's life turned
into a petting zoo—this he cannot take.

I have become like my mother where I don't
need sleep in a new city anymore; immune
to time shifts, I just wander and buy fruit
and almonds and a good loaf
of bread and today, some fresh juice, skipping museums
though I want to go back to see Anne Frank's

house this time, because this time,
I am a woman and last time, I was a girl
and when you are a girl, all you see is another girl
and when you are a woman, all you see is history
careering towards a girl whom you cannot protect.

In my Amsterdam apartment, I find a ceramic plate
with its rim edge folded in five places and a violet petal
has been painted at its compression. In it, I pour
some olive oil and a little bit of salt and sit
on the white couch overlooking
the neon-green blooms gathering on a branch
outside the large window directly facing an apartment
of a bookish couple, the kind who forget
they have bodies and think they are better
than those who are bodily
which is most everyone else.
But the girl in the couple is lying
and misses the small animal inside her
crying for breakfast.
What she needs is food, not Yeats.
What she needs is your fingers.
The apartment has tulips and pink Depression glass
and cacti of all heights like skyscrapers.

I am thinking of Harlem in Amsterdam.
Sometimes I go there to hide.
I go there to eat at a bistro owned by a lady
named Fay. In Harlem, there is Fay
and she is older with light eyes and her whole
family owns this place and her grandson works
behind the bar and he's just seventeen and a soccer
player and this week got into Dartmouth and I ask
if she thinks he'll be happy, being a black
kid at Dartmouth, but Fay is Queen Fay
and knows better than to answer questions
about race at dinnertime especially in front
of all these nice people.

In Amsterdam, the cold sunlight of April
grows the dandelions in the gutter and when
you get to 263 to see Anne Frank's house
(only from the outside) the building is not as tall
as you remember and you wonder what the ceilings
were like for a young girl and you imagine
her face, I imagine her face and think
maybe something bad happened to Josh
when he was a kid and you see her
face in the window, her face lit up in story,
her face in love and in fear, and you are in Amsterdam
when the American president bombs Syria.

You say American president as if you are not
an American and as if he is not your president.
You promised that he would not make his way
into any poem, but here he is bombing
Syria and here he is in your poem
and here is her face spreading all over
Europe and here is your face, Anne,
spreading all over Europe and here is
your face, your face, your face.

DIOR

When she picked up the *NY Times*,
mother made a comment:

Good for you.

Mother was a mean bear.

When sister was nine, mother pulled her **hair**
to the ground because she couldn't spell **a word right.**

Sister was like a stunk fish
when her face, bangs-first, hit the floor.

My god, that woman
could make a weapon

out of anything:

Tylenol bottles. Cheerios box.

A few strands of black
in the thick of her paw.

FABRIC IN TRIBECA

We are buying curtains to cover up my life.
We are buying patterns to cover up my lethargia.
My sadness is very adult. You can bring it to places
in public and it will not make a scene.
You will not be embarrassed by it.
It will not act out, but only wander, slightly undisciplined.
Look at the red inverted-enteric shapes spit across the silk,
endlessly unfolding into our arms. Six dollars for the uneven pieces.
This should do the trick, the leftover cloth
that promises to distort the incoming winter
light into something bearable.
Who buys fabric in January?
Who makes curtains to give their sadness a perimeter?

The clerks speak Yiddish and look at us like pregnant dolls,
and we are all here deciphering one another
in the drowsy New York afternoon.
Judith says we need to go. She needs to get to Mikvah by five.
Twenty dollars to be cleansed.
The monthly baptism for women who bleed, for women who carry.
Even now, inside her, the baby is stirring to the ring of our voices,
the underwater radio where everyone sounds as if they are choking.

I think she'll be a tomboy and extend her childhood across
the universe, a little gender deviant for the stars.
All that matters is if you're Jewish, the owner says, and I smile
and press the paisley linen to my face.
We need to go, Judith repeats. *I need to be clean.*
I look at my treasures, neatly folded, and wonder
if I am talented enough to do anything
worthwhile with these hands.

WHITE PEOPLE ALWAYS WANT TO TELL ME THAT THEY GREW UP POOR

White people don't like when
you say:

white people.

White people
like to remind you

that you are Indian, not black.

Black people
never say that to you.

They make
a home for you

inside
their archives.

It is like an elegy.

Poverty must be
a color

but color
is like sky.

My daddy is a daddy from Africa.
An Indian boy from Tanga.

He is a papa

who stitches
eyes together—

a doctor, the only
one

of his siblings,

seventeen in all,
to really get out

and climb towards

the lands
that enslaved him.

Only white people

can imagine a past
that was better

than now.

Only white people get
to have

nostalgia.

You grew up rich, they say.
Your daddy is a doctor.

They want me

to possess
their whiteness, too.

They want
to spread it

outwards
like the tentacles of

a squid.

What they are really
saying is:

How dare you
have what was rightfully mine.

I want to say:
Squid,

my daddy holds storms
from a world you've never seen.

He is a doctor
because

it was a way
to unbury

his dead.

I want to say:
It is not me you hate.

It is that you were
not given what whiteness

promised you—

what your TV said
all white people could have.

My daddy didn't have a TV.
My daddy is from Africa.

My daddy is not a thing like your daddy.
Our house was not a thing like your house.

Our household was not held by anything

you could name. If you swam in it,
you wouldn't even know

it was water.

NUKEMAP.COM

It is 2:37 AM and I make myself eat an apple while on the laptop,
Alec Baldwin is hosting *Match Game*, an experiment in the ageless art
of game show hosting, like orange light diving back into the '70s.
In an open tab, I am dropping nukes on New York City
to watch the airburst swell into a new species of hydrogen fruit. I do this
over and over until each bomb becomes a son that you detonate virtually
into the night: Davy Crockett and Little Boy, Fat Man and Ivy Mike,
Gadget, Castle Bravo and Tsar Bomba, all of the bombs
are named for boys with fathers from Pakistan and Russia,
sly America or the green seawaters of a Korean dream.
Some of the really bad nukes only have numbers
and are unnameable like B83 because you can't name something
that can kill 1.8 million people
even if you are its mother.

You detonate the bomb and listen to "Gravity Rides Everything."
You detonate the bomb and still think the '90s will save you.
You tell your roommate that if the bomb goes off above 39th,
you might both survive.
New York City is the default target on nukemap.com.
This is so unquestioned that you clutch your O'Hara
and handwrite David Trinidad a letter in Chicago
to tell him about nuke anxiety. He doesn't even know you well,
but he was nice once in the lobby of the Marlton on 8th Street when you
recited Creeley and talked for three hours and lately
you only want to be around people over sixty.

You still expect them to save you. You still believe in elders.
You can get the second season of *Match Game* on ABC.com for free.
You can watch all your favorite comedians from 1992 come to life,
resurrected like clay prophets, saying that you can live
in the television where nothing will incinerate you.
You are back in Seinfeld's apartment and all that matters
is that Jerry doesn't want to date someone with man hands.
All our futures are like time beating backwards into sitcoms
with the laugh tracks of the dead, and the apple in your mouth is now
an organism you slew in your throat and each of your sons—
Davy and Mike and Bravo and Fat Man—are standing
on top of a heap of nuclear soil
that was once a very specific girl, let's call her Ana,
and they are asking you to forgive them
like any mother would.

HOW HAVE YOU PREPARED FOR YOUR DEATH?

—after Bhanu Kapil

I get on planes.
Each time

I board, I knock
the metal.

Turbulence fore-
cast. Severe

winds
over Colorado.

I map
the storms

of the whole world.

BAD HABIT

We are in Vermont. We are in New Hampshire.
We are in all the states where loss is white,
where cars dance towards their ends
across small highways going south.
All I do is mourn you all over the countrysides,
both French and Californian,
and surely some unspoken nations of wilderness in between.
All the four-legged deer look like you
with their lemur eyes, uncovered
from the soil loosening around their skulls,
a graveyard of doe ankles
sticking up in crisscrosses in a field
and all of them are you, all of them are the kinks,
those anonymous songs you played
on car rides through the LA fog
before arriving in Santa Barbara
and I thought we'd both die there, gently
skidding off the 101 into the ocean, and I always
think of that day on particularly bad Christmases,
you know, the sorrowful ones.
You will tell me there were happy ones, too.
I am a bad person who is acting badly.
You are sleeping somewhere.
You are sleeping with the gazelles,
with the kid we never had,
the one you never came with me to end,

the one you said I overindulged.
You are with the Kinks
playing on a record in an abandoned field
with dead deer and no blood, just the stateless fog moving in
to make it all invisible
even though we know what is there.
What I learned most from you is how
to be a body that does not react,
to play dead in an unearned paradise.
What I learned from you is how
not to be a body.

HOW TO SAY CONGRATULATIONS—
I'M SORRY—WHO ARE YOU NOW

I send flowers to all the women I love. To Cassandra,
when she got her PhD from Harvard in entomology working

with the butterfly professor with the nice smile.
To my aunt, who can't really stand me and hasn't since I thought

I was smarter than everyone. To my mother, whom I never call enough,
but who is silenced by the gesture of gloomy red-faced ruscus

arriving at her door. I want to blow cold flower heads into the season
have them show up in piles, overwhelm the side-cracked steps

and oak porches of women across the globe, especially in a Boston winter.
I want those petunia heads to die slowly in the dirty snow

like pink gravestones, muddled with aggression, choosing to finally wilt
only in the audacity of day. I want to send a love that feels hard to them.

I want them to use thorns in battle, choke with allergies, resurrect old
lovers in a porcelain bathtub, dull their husbands and children

with sour blankets of petals until everything in their house is a decaying
color that can exist only in nature, until every cardinal direction they look,

they get to swoon and swoon and swoon and become a vortex
of dizzy neglect. I want those stargazer lilies to flirt and accuse:

Congratulations. I'm sorry. Who are you now.

FIVE OF SWORDS

My first real tarot reading and already, it is telling me what I know too well. These swords are supposed to mean my intellect is killing me but it reads more like a failure of femininity, a coldness to raise the brows, and why are there worms on this card, all these struggling decapitated worms? How am I ever supposed to get on the subway after this? I wonder how an entomologist would read this card with its serpentine arthropods that supposedly mean self-destruction or self-renewal and in the meantime, my friend, Catherine the Blonde over here, gets a bunch of cups and unicorns and harmony and something that signals water and emotional health and a book deal and all her dreams coming true and some card with a dainty fawn or some shit on it and here I am with my worms and a lamb that looks like it's about to be stabbed five times.

I tell two men I love about this reading and they both chalk it up to "interpretation" which is so like them to try and mollify the inevitable. One researches tarot online, convinced the reading is somehow about him, and the other shrugs, convinced that nothing (especially nothing to do with me) could ever be about him and I talk this over with Grits and Franklin, two New England goats down the road with absolutely no horse in the race, but their lack of bias just feels like indifference and this is why people should not leave the city and go to Connecticut, the underworld of all your disbelief.

I remember the time Jeff was so convinced an earthquake was going to tumble LA that he packed up his cat and flew them both to the East Coast and we all laughed at him when the psychic who told him to flee was called out on the news for causing mass hysteria and I remember thinking how susceptible he was and now I think, how sad, really, and also, how silly we all are trying to avoid the disobedient fates, and since I hate flying and oceans, the earth is where I want to be and want to die, with those worms and fated lambs who are so delicious and yet when you ordered a rack of it at a restaurant, I just wept over the tiny body until I gathered myself insisting *it is nothing, nothing, I'm sorry, I'm leaving and I eat lamb all the time and what was my problem* and maybe you were right, maybe it was about you all along.

THE EULOGY

Once, you told me about art class
at the cancer center and said sometimes
you start with twelve but end with only nine.
This is common, you shrug—and your voice
becomes hoarse and hoarseness is not dread,
it is exhaustion nested in the bottom rung of
your spine and when I am with you,
I feel like a person who hardly knows
how to be a person anymore.

By the Pacific, everyone is trying.
Sand is more beautiful than stars, I say, if you look
under a scope, you can see rhino horns, cacti,
a Peruvian lover. After, you shrug.
After, you die.
After, your father is starting to look thin.
Your friends tend to your grapefruit trees.
Your sister and I sit at a gay bar and don't speak
and someone says to your mother: *It must have been so hard.*

When I hear this, I want to take my fist to a mountain
and pound the surface until five men I have loved
pull me away, and in this dream, they all get along,
and retreat to their separate gardens where I can visit.
Here, all the gardens are English and all the men
I have loved tell me the things I want to hear except

you, who have no garden, whom I did not enchant,
who says I am an imposter. Tell me all the things
I didn't want to hear. *Narcissist. Liar. Pretty Bitch.*
You wouldn't have said any of it, of course.
Even if you had survived.

WHY WE DRINK

I tell Malik I'm going to stop. I tell him that I do it
because I am sad and because someone
was mean to me at a lecture after five men
spoke during the Q&A so I said something, finally,
about energy and petrocultures and didn't the infrastructure
of the moon landing look just like the oil fields
of Alberta and some older Italian man said no, said I was
projecting as if projection were not interpretation
but it was in front of a lot of people and what
was the point of all my degrees and giving up a decade
of life to school if I could be so easily humiliated and maybe
I shouldn't have worn jeans shredded at my thighs
or that navy sweater, sleeves blooming with moth holes
but if these are our Left institutions, if these are the men
on our side, I said, then of course, I am going to drink.

Malik tells me you can't quit before thirty-five
because you're not going to stay quit
and something about me trusts him because
he was at the Ear Inn back when it was the Ear Inn,
back in the old New York and he tells me I am
the new New York and I don't even know how
to tell him that I am not even that.
I say, humiliation is like the nausea of childhood with
those delayed epiphanies. I hate the violence of insight—
the lesson is always how one is ugly or dishonest,
the shortcomings that could build a civilization and then did.

Malik is not even so much older, forty-something, but there have been
many Maliks and therefore he claims ancientness. He says it's all real.
My parents and those men and yes, even the feeble species.
He keeps a notebook and writes down all the great Irish bits
spiraling out of Helen's mouth at dinner. He sits cross-legged
on a pillow, cradles lemons and snacks on pickle, waxes poetic
while he assesses the spice level of a green Peruvian sauce I make
which he ranks only a three for spice but insists
it is a ten in taste because he knows I am fragile.
He does impressions of nutritionists and people who get jazzed
about gym memberships but I know, though we are laughing,
that he is really sad. Sad that this is the theater of his multitasking,
that the corruptions are multiplying faster than our jokes
so we have become creatures who can slip through
dimensions, our times thick with simultaneity, so ready
we are to be brutalized many times a day. Even with laughter.
Malik says maybe it's time to leave New York. He can tell
we're all getting tilted there, and by that he means
becoming products, paralyzed by false moonlight in the streets.

I tell Malik I drink because I am tired and because they hate us anyway
and we are outside while others smoke at the opening
of The Red Wheelbarrow in Paris and I'm wearing a polka-dot dress
and I forgot to put on a bra this morning and it is freezing
and I see myself, the mess of my complaints and temperatures, the way
I am not making any sense these days. He says yes and yes and yes.
He keeps saying it is all okay, all real, tells me to turn my insights
into continents, into paintings. Get sloppy, delicate. Be a feral amateur.
When I get back to New York, he is the only one I still talk to on the regular.
He says "Listen to this" and "Read this" and his brain is so addicted to joy
and we both get nominated for a prize in the same week and it works
it really does work, the way his spirit skims octaves across the ocean
into my heart, into this poem, the way he said my Jesus year
now that I'm thirty-three is going to reveal something about me
which it just did and do you know, this time the revelation
didn't hurt so much. Which is what Malik might call aging,
a process not nearly as dire as they want you to believe.

BELLEVILLE

When I don't finish
the pho noodles

collecting
in the hot broth

you look at me
and say

that I must never
have been poor

though
what you mean

is that I have never
gone hungry.

Never had to whore
myself out

to a couple
looking

for a good time
while in Paris

for a few
days.

I sit quietly
as you finish

your meal
not knowing if

I am to eat now or not.
Instead, I gulp

the Mexican beer
you ordered

and think of oranges
and organs

stomachs
and hearts and how

you cannot
discern

between them
anymore.

I sit like a daisy.
You assess me like a king

trying to make up
his mind, steam rising

from our bowls—
a drama

we can ill afford.
I get it, I say.

You feast
on what you can.

RUNNING IN THE SUBURBS

by the truck with the Trump bumper sticker
and since you do a loop around these shaded streets,
you always smile at everyone. You don't look like
a threat, but maybe someone's nanny here.
Maybe someone's maid. What is the maid doing
running around in circles on our block, they are
thinking. What is the maid trying to stay fit for?
Everything, even your smile, becomes a little
more criminal. You want to utter things that make
you ashamed. You want to recite them Dickinson
and Poe, challenge their knowledge of Barolo wines.
You are such an insecure petite bourgeoise
and how quickly you became one, from being
broke when cheddar was a luxury, stuck in tens
of thousands of student debt to now, the professor
who runs while in residence at a writers' colony.
You're still in debt, kid. You're still brown.
They still think you are the nanny or maid.
Your twenty-year-old self is still laughing at you.
The guesswork keeps building even when there is sun
a few deer making eye contact, the brilliant blue sky,
Dinah Washington crying rivers in your headphones.
You tell your mom about running in this suburb
and she is annoyed: *Not everything is about race, Megan.*
She has shit to do today—elder care, a doctor's visit.
She's got no time for my hypotheses. *I know,* I say.

Defensive. Ashamed. I ask her how she is finally,
but I hear a voice reversing us in my head. It says:
Not everything is about race, Mama.
Not everything is about race.

REGRET IS A BLUE DIVE

I know regret bakes hot.
It begins with coffee,
the supple drug
everyday like
firewood in your hands
birch, broken,
a slanted piece of wood stuck
in the knuckle ridge of your skin
that you carry on the NYC train running
uptown to share with your neighbor,
a stranger, so happy you are to not
live in a Jersey suburb but to eat cardamom
panna cotta and coffee and pretend
wealth, pretend youth, staring at
the bridges that all your favorite poets
threw themselves from and at least
once every few months you look up
how to hang yourself because it is actually hard
to snap your neck at the best angle and then
you feel shitty about it because there
was a boy, a student at the school
where you teach, who walked into a forest one day
and did not come out.

You might have to deal with the fact
that you will never be a mother.
Let that sink in. You might have to acknowledge
that you might never have been
a very good one and so it is probably
no real loss and anyway, you read queer theory
and NO FUTURE or something like
no conceivable future though you're pretty sure
you've conceived once or twice, that hot trail
of blood running to your knees on the hotel bathroom floor
in Milwaukee where you wondered if it was more than
what it was and the planet is swinging
outwards on a gravity vine and wouldn't
be here for your grandkids anyway though you're pretty sure
your grandkids would like the internet
and did you know if you google
how to hang yourself, the internet is kind.
I am surprised that the internet cares, routing me
to hotlines, wooing me with titles like:
"If you only read one thing, read this" and I read it
and it actually isn't very good, not for me,
too mathematical, something about depression
on a scale of bending resources. I read Jack Spicer
instead and that helps except nothing helped Jack Spicer
when he drank himself into a San Francisco ward
and I wonder what percentage of people

who read that article think:
this math is the savage math that will save me.
Depression is an endless Quebec snowfield,
it is the Pacific Ocean in January, whaleless
and deep in soft, cold current.

Things that are brave are often painful,
I'm not sure why we do them, really, and things
that are brave don't often look brave and maybe won't
for two hundred years—
I forgot to say that in addition to not being a mother,
you might just be alone. Sit with that. Think of those joys,
the form of solo waltz you will dance around
your bed quilt, the trance of your morning drift,
how you will learn to make dinner just for one mouth,
how you will learn to feed only yourself
and how it will not be sad at all.

II

GOOD BOYS

Once in a car, a good boy
shook me hard. *If you like it*
that way in bed, then why are you...
the tiny bruises on my arms
where his prints pressed into my pink
sleeves rose to the surface like rattles.
Like requests. They thrived there
for a week until they settled
into a wet blackness.
A bruise can sweeten your blood,
can bloom the sweetness into you.
A bruise can bloom rabbits like pines.
Once in a car, everything between us
started growing. And then I was not
in the car or the state
or the East Coast anymore.
I was at the summit of a prayer
reeling from an animal mouth,
my tongue an unseeable act,
because, here is the truth:
Even the good boys
want to shake you down, want to come
in your mouth and hair, want to quake
above you if only
for a moment. *Come home.*

Come home, another good boy says.
I would never shake you. I would never
do anything to your body.

NIGHT WALK ON LONG ISLAND

Mid-August. The moody Northeast.
Yellow moon undressing

herself in the bay. Shelter Island
all asleep. Turpentine skies

cooled by faint meteors,
a shower of bashful stars.

Virgil, in my ribcage, singing
to the sweet red-cedar scent.

Virgil, in my ribcage, singing.

AT THE PUBLIC LIBRARY, SURROUNDED BY THE UNLIKELY IN MONTAUK, NY

I am being interrogated by all the things I do not believe in, like my dead
aunts and uncles arriving at a party as if they are not dead.

The way interracial couples have sex is always a bit complicated,
reenacting histories in our beds, not all of them massacres, but each of us

has an addiction to scenes of red seen in grade school, late-night HBO,
that art palace in Chicago when we stood transfixed, unsettled, newly wed.

The librarians downstairs are talking about Keanu Reeves and there are
finance guys who stopped in from the beach to charge their laptops

and check to see how the market is wavering a quarter point today.
These people make me so sad—like trembling weeds, as if the most

precise insult might kill them outright, but hey, even I am in the library
to redeem myself. Coming here is like going to confession, the forgiveness

is smug which is almost every kind of forgiveness, but you cannot redeem
yourself if you groan too much. Thoreau said camels are the only

animals that can "ruminate" while walking, in an essay dictated
from his deathbed to his younger sister, Sophia.

He said that he always walks towards Oregon, not Europe, and that the
compass of a nation is built then on how to take hills going West,

which is, I think, also known as Manifest Destiny.
Which is, I'm sure, also known as genocide.

PHONE CALL IN THE TREES

So as to not disturb
the thin walls,

I carry your voice
into the woods,

amid the aromatic,
twisting evergreens.

One always remembers
the scenes in which

the heart moves.
Leaves droop

to greet me as the details
of your mornings

and twilights
travel like seeds

arriving by the jaws
of gulls. Bunnies, small

and unafraid, chew grass
too close, rubbing

their cheeks in the purple
marsh blazing stars.

That we live with
such tender scales

and gatherings
is a testament

to a kind wildness.
Three states west

of here, your voice
ascends,

feeding on sour
treetops.

And above, clouds

strangled with moisture
refuse to burst.

VENUS, AGED

When you talk in circles,
it reminds me of Lonnie Johnson.
You make small imitations of my voice.
You turn my pout into a little character.
Like a children's book. Like the one about a tiger
who came to tea right at a child's bedtime.
I let you do things. I let you order.
I tell you about the tumors
singing to each other in my mother's brain.
You say something about your sun, the son,
the moonless spitting in the night,
your sadness like a cradled apricot
in the palm of my hands. Your hands are rough
when I cup them, we compare lines—
all healthy heartbreaks etched across our lunar palms,
all captive pathways of animals
and hairlines we have loved.

What is a line anyways. A small horizon of age.
A pursuit. Your leg gently in rest, the sweet citrus
of drink between us. The air is vulnerable.
Any small tease might hurt so we are careful
with each other's pasts. We mostly talk
about what is in front of us which is nothing
we can really have, which must exist parallel
to the lives we have built like a rabbit's ear
blushing in the night, the blood shooting
upwards to its apex, its heaven,
the twin celestial leaves atop its head.

Here I am, your crisis in white.
With flowers up and down my dress.
With a gold cuff digging into my arm.
What part of our bodies are not fauna.
What part of us is actually here.

THE JUNGLE

In midsummer, in Los Angeles,
the night is fractured

with mountains, grilling ink
into the blue thaw. I trail

into pools and pastures,
and in the diner,

tattoos speck
and skirt up booths,

the waitress, Dottie, is whipping
shells, mac and cheese,

waffles and chickens,
all oracles in the oil.

You think I'm kidding? Look
at Hopper's orange rooms,

his lone man. Vineyards
are boring to paint,

the coffee rumbling us all
into a primal scene, the mismatched

silverware like guns in a western,
all the possibilities

of a warm night.
The thing about LA

Is anyone can walk through
the door. The drunk drive,

open-air and clipping down
Highland Avenue.

Here are all the streets
I remember:

Alvarado and Effie.
Mohawk and Montana.

Before all this?

The hills of Carpinteria,
cattle punk, the drained floodplains

and eucharistic jimson weed.
But dig that ditch city,

those impersonal stones,
the great vigilance

of the 19th century,
the circus of eggs on the plate,

Dottie full of lips, just lips
sipping, stinging the sandy air.

SONORA

I read Hannah's book to learn how coyotes can be baited
off path with a piece of bloodied meat in a ziplock bag.
About why aliens always land in the desert because it looks
so hygienic and why teenagers keep ending up dead
next to cacti erected like crucifixes in the night.
I saw just one ghost when I was little, rocking in a chair
next to my bed, a pioneer lady with a bonnet. She told me to meet her
on the tire swing in the daylight but never had the nerve to show.
As a kid, I had a blond imaginary friend named Jenny who
wore a red-collared white dress. I gave her my bed one night
because she was my guest and I didn't want to be rude.
I was hallucinating white women everywhere—so deferential
to their graceful, immaterial bodies, their cooing requests, the demure
fashion that hid a lust for conquest. I slept on the ground of my closet
like a servant. When I was found, it was sweet distress.
My parents held hands, relieved that no man had come for the youngest
child of the only dark-bodied family in a radius of miles and miles
from this Albertan suburb. What would I have done if I were them?
Whom would I have accused? I went missing a few times as a child
and I always wanted a trophy when I was found, as if there were credit
to be given for being discernible. Hannah writes about how curses spread
best between the narrow chop of mountains and valleys, suicides
multiplying due to weather—the inside of wind, a voice
telling you where the pistol is kept, lightning like ibuprofen.
In Arizona, all the Starbucks feel haunted
and people get haircuts as a way to time travel. It's the kind

of book that follows you around afterwards, where you try to shake it off by drinking too much coffee and then masturbating or walking barefoot on a small, stony overgrowth of a stranger's driveway in Montauk, NY, hoping the imprint massaging your underfoot will knead the spells out of your ever-thickening blood, knotting itself into a gentle exorcism.

IT'S GETTING DARK. IT'S GOING TO RAIN.
—after William Carlos Williams

Every time I bike to the sea,
I feel there is a chance I won't come back.

Each animal in my path
appears like a foreshadowing—

the foreboding mist, a loose helmet,
my jangled knees pushing up the hill,

coasting past cemeteries and sand-swept
playgrounds, courts without nets, many trucks

sailing too close to the grass.
Which is why every outing feels

like a sacred risk, a voyage

in which I want to kiss and call the people
who would feel my absence most.

I start to make the list but stop
to see the sea peeking above a roll

in the mossy road.

I start to make the list
in my head but stop.

COLORING HOUR

Joan Baez, paralyzed in sunlight. And there is too much
sand in the washing machine from the beach fire last night,
the grains refusing to lose mass in their usual tumult of water.
I listen to military experts on North Korea and realize what a sucker
I am for the calm, strategic violence in the voice
of an older man. As if information mattered anymore.
I go for a run in a cemetery. I don't think the dead mind.
I do a yoga video in my room to the sound of a nice lady
who now lives in California with three children.
She bends in the video and laughs softly, encourages child's pose.
I am a beginner at yoga. I am a beginner at most things.
I wonder if she's worried about her children right now.
If they decide to bomb, I will have to walk into the ocean
at the End-of-the-World, probably alone, and put stones in my pockets
like Virginia and just keep walking. I go talk to the ladies
at Seniors' Coloring Hour at the library. There is Joyce whom I like
in particular, and we use water-soluble colored pencils, making the blues
so blue and pinks so pink. Joyce tells me about how the submarines
used to be stationed out here during WWII and the torpedo would throw
them into the air like muscular whales that slam back into the ocean
after an enthusiastic jump. Joyce's husband was a structural engineer
for NASA and used to fly to Houston. He was in charge
of making the rockets land. *It's hard for things to be both strong and light*,
she tells me proudly. I ask her if she is more afraid now than before.
She says it feels more like WWII than Vietnam.
She keeps telling me this is a great country even when

I cry about my sister in Charlottesville. I am crying here
among all these women over eighty. I am ruining coloring hour
for seniors at the library. I need so many mothers. I am a youngest child.
I need all these women between me and the world. These women
and my own mother and both my sisters and when they invite me back
next week, I feel a little sheepish, but I take home my painting,
which is my version of Matisse's *The Piano Lesson*
and I prop it up on my desk and feel full of a torrential love.

SICILIA

When it appears on your arm
like a map, you go to choke the green leaf
thinking *poison ivy* or *poison oak*
and that makes you think of Uma Thurman
in Batman while the spire of red bumps creeps
around your elbows and knees, the joints
always being the first crevices to quarantine,
as if your skin were the site of plagues.
More and more, you think green is a color
you will have to commit to memory—
the first emission of light to go extinct,
people's hazel eyes rolling out of their
sockets, the myrtle trees pushing their arms
back into the ground, growing muscle bark,
the seas ossifying into stone.

I have dreams about Ginostra, a town of forty-five
off the coastal lip of Stromboli, where I watched
a slaughtered swordfish get rolled up a hill,
where sour capers filled the space
between my cheeks and gums,
where a biblical rain swept across
the Tyrrhenian Sea towards us
and before this, I must admit, I didn't know
that water had feet, flogging the surface
like Hermes, who found humans

such a nuisance, and who at the right moment,
with the right bait, could come for you
with Icarian terror and speed.

THE EDWARD ALBEE BARN

I write you letters, but lately also like to make you diagrams of buildings
in which I have walked, showing you the entryway, the window where

I saw a steely rabbit, the yawning of an open barn door. I am getting better
at drawing stairs and hallways, labeling old wall phones and record players,

soon the diagram becomes so detailed that each bookcase must give you at
least five titles so you understand the personality of a room.

Here are the dried lavender and the free weights and the tree spores
and the lone tennis racket. Here is the outlet where I was electrocuted

when the case came off my phone charger and my thumb bruised black
and then callused, where I learned that burn creams work on both

electrical and solar scalds. This is the BBQ, I note, where I wrapped a sweet
potato in foil and heated it until it became utter mush.

Here's where I planted thyme, but it was too late and it wouldn't grow.
Here is where I speak to you on the phone and ask about your mother and

then your grandmother and then you ask about my mother and all the
mothers. Here is the green picnic table and upstairs, a desk

where I obsessively write you letters and stick them in blue envelopes
and bike them downtown to the one postbox and watch them get eaten up.

MODERN NATION-STATES

People always think Canada is the answer and America, the beast.
But I saw how they make beasts in Sicily

and how they need to grow for centuries on top of salt flatlands
and salt mountains. Don't let the shallow seas fool you—

the Mediterranean has the oldest seafloor in the world,
at least 280 million years of ancient ocean between Africa and Europe,

disappearing into a crust. I drink in a town of notable ruins
since the Belice earthquake of 1968 and I am listening to people

teach me about Sicilian volcanoes and Sicilian politics
which go together. An older lady said that in Gibellina, a woman

named Anna was cleaning the church steps when the first tremor
occurred and a piece of the cathedral just fell off.

She never said if it fell on Anna, but ran to her father's orchard
with her children who only brought their Christmas shoes

and what they don't say enough about earthquakes
is the way the shocks continue to build, how one minute you are sitting

next to your brother and the next, in the violent shake and dust,
he is across the room. The old town of Gibellina was turned into art.

Which is to say that it was turned really into a graveyard when a
contemporary artist filled its half-standing homes with concrete

until it looked like a lunar sarcophagus, white and labyrinthine,
where the trapped dead still push out caper vines and even the birds,

flying above, pause in reverence. In Sicily, I listen to a boy
from Argentina tell me what America looks like, and it looks ugly.

At home, I like the way my Brazilian friend, Aarão, is afraid
to go out on his balcony on the 24th floor of a building

on the Upper East Side, that the threat of the ledge is sickening,
that he laughs when I tell him his view would be the best

to watch the downfall of a civilization. This is our mood these days,
which is, I'm told, very American—

to think in catastrophes, to stretch in disaster, to make events
more shark-like, to eat up trash. This summer, people all over the world

tell me about the country called America and yet I do not know to what
they refer. I shrug. I get worked up. I shrug again.

All I know is that in Paris, white men don't look at me and in Lisbon,
people still cherish children and in Palermo, I watch my close friend, Elisa,

roll and smoke cigarette after cigarette amid the Mafia windmills.
In Montreal, when I walk in a store, no one will help me

like in *Pretty Woman*, and in New York, you can fall in and out of love
in the same day with a cheap, fickle quickness that was once defined

as so Roman and now is so very reactionary. So very American.
Yet, to be from here is to always underreact.

Even if it kills you. Even if the flooding waters have already snuck
through the screen door, soaked the carpet, swelled your feet.

It is to deny all of it even at the moment when your family
is drowning. Truly, nothing is exceptional here

except that my parents looked at a map and leapt and were received
on some days and on others, not at all. Like everywhere.

WHAT WILL YOU MISS ABOUT THE EARTH?
—*after Bhanu Kapil*

That it spun.
That everything was a portrait of gravity.

The smell of a new body, newly close,
ready to love.

MANCHESTER TO LISBON

In seat 15B, she begins to pray in Portuguese. On her lap, a magazine pink with tips about cellulite, hair weaves, and some gossip about Mrs. Clooney. We are both nervous, but I tell her it's OK, my mother was a flight attendant for Saudi Arabian Airlines back in the day, and I know all the signs of what could go wrong: tight coffee-lip of the hostess, rush for the jump seat, that stuck choking sound of jammed landing gear. The woman doesn't understand, but takes my swollen, bruised hand like a blade of ginger and holds it in hers. We pray until the shaking metal sinks into a soft cruise. I learn that the man sitting in 15A is her husband and wonder at the indifference to her address. I wonder why she chose my hand, an unbeliever, a fallen woman with at least six band-aids covering wounds from an uncontrolled night. My mother once had to slap her colleague out of hysterics when flying over Doha. *There is nothing we can do*, she snapped. So like her. The calm, shrewd violence. The cruelness that could keep you alive.

CALYPSO IN PARIS

It is a hideous November—

even your
indifference

takes a blue form.

You are for the new world,
tomorrow.

I, for America, today.

Your apartment is cold
and I search your kitchen

for napkins

as you bite into
a late-night animal.

You wake

to tell me
about a dream

of us eating out

someone
together.

I want to ask

but don't.
I have given myself

seven hours of flight

to bring
my halves back

as one—

though the body is a dull metaphor,
won't quite line up.

Part of me

has already
departed,

the other sits

motionless,
blows ash off the windowsill

and small curls

of burning paper
descend,

doomed
for the fruit stands below.

It is a hideous November—

birds glide down the canal,
strings

of city wires

slope like hills, fluid
and tapered

by wind.

THE POET HOLDS A GUN

The bullet is a simple, adolescent heartache.
When guns go off around you, you wince like a single sheet
and nothing in your body has ever been so simultaneous
not even orgasm which is more like the hungry sea
meeting an Aeolian beach with its sweet
caper storms and prickly pear trees. An orgasm
has more surface area and salt than a gun.

On the ride home from the range, from the first lesson,
I ask Alex if he wants to have a baby
and he explains the mathematical formula
for a circle tattooed across his wrist. He doesn't
mention that I am bad at holding a gun
or that I gasp every time I press
the trigger while my wrist flaps back like a muscle
from another life, or that I look like a meek captive,
or that he could tell, without saying
a word, that I was begging for him to take it
out of my hands. He doesn't mention the baby and it feels
like the small relief of passover when he gently
takes the gun and hits the target seven times
in a row, perfectly. We don't talk about
how we are both from the sterile Main Line
of Philly where the only big bookstore shut down across
from a milk-shake shop, that we are suburban astronauts
who just shot at a paper-plate target
like a white, punctured moon.

The poet holds a gun in the morning
and shakes, with the same fallen limb,
the knowing hand of Agnès Varda that very night
in New York where the faces of her film
beam the most affectionate kind of love
which is love without sound or dialogue.
Varda is a small woman, sharp like a radiant heat
dressed in magenta, a ring of Saturn
around her head and she is telling me
something about my hand when she shakes it:

Megan, she seems to say the name that never meant
anything to me but who she knows
(and my mother knows) is very much me.
There is nothing here to defend and everyone is in love.
Here, her hand says, *Megan, you do not need the gun.*

CONVERSION

sam says you can't name your book *good boys* without a dog
but sam doesn't know that i am the dog
i am the ultimate mutt and i am telling him this story
at the bar called college hill tavern which looks like a front
for some operation where all the bar stools appear as if
they were staged in under ten minutes and
the girl with the fake lashes knows
i like a double gin and i am telling sam
that i am a dog who was converted
when i was seventeen and my mother found an essay
about how i was in love with a girl
and there was a portishead reference
in case you need me to date it
and this was way before the liberation of the young and the white
twins on youtube who come out to their dad
and everybody cries and transforms.
when i see those kids all i think is that they never had parents
who were immigrants and who sent you to a lady
and told you that you had to solve it all
in one session because this therapy was expensive.
it wasn't so traumatic. rather funny. and i remember the couch
there were multiple couches and i had to choose a spot and i sat
on the couch farthest from her and this wasn't the first nice lady
who looked at me like i was a dog
and sam, when i said it is called good boys
what i meant was that i was a good boy

and loved good boys
and good men and still love them
but you see, i was seventeen and alone
and nobody gave me anything except one book by dickinson
and she was so neat, so precise, so human
and i wasn't. i just wasn't.
i was just a dog. i wasn't even that good.

III

SCYLLA AND CHARYBDIS

I like when the choices are both ugly—
the rock and the hard place. Odysseus chose
Scylla and I too would have opted for
a terrestrial evil, the sea vortex probably
concealing some subterranean meat with its beauty.
Soon you and I will exist in different time zones.
While day breaks for you, night will hold me to the big, wild moon.
I cast a wakeful light unraveling across the ocean.
While you swim in open Spanish waters brushing
the bright-eyed fish, I spin in a street of yellow cars
nod off to an organ in a small church on Broadway.
When you face the queen medusas in the water
transfixed by their pale rosy pulses
their accusatory look of afterlife—know that you are facing me.
I am them in hundreds, blind and mutant
ready to greet and interrogate your days.
These hallucinations are such a small price for your face.
I keep myself busy and disoriented.
I trace our disappearing homelands through myth.
I understand now that to love radically is to always
be willing to be banished to some disfigured island of stone
in the middle of the sea, a small sacrifice, really.
I, too, might have sacrificed a few men
to preserve the whole idea of a voyage.
Or even a nation. Both false beloveds.
That's the thing.

Our hero didn't really want to go down with the ship.
Wily, he skidded the sea cosmos.
He knew the milk foaming at the whirlpool's edge
was bad medicine and chose the lesser of two omens—
a prophecy where the weak get plucked
and you sail on home fine. Just fine.

NIGHT, THE FIRST

Little Apollo, what can I say.
I want you in my bed all the time.
I want you climbing out of my desk.
I want you to tell me the story again
about the giant who talks conspiracies
or how you got those lacerations on your back.
No. I don't want to know about that.
Or where you slept last night
when I was drinking myself
into the peak spring grass of McCarren park.
We joke about such dark things
as if treachery were exquisite.
As if stamping the night with traps
means we might have nothing
to face in the morning.
At the botanical garden, we pause
in front of a lattice dome of orchids,
yellow and perched, canaries in crisscross.
You ask me what is the point
of such indulgent beauty.
I tell you that these are altars.
That indulgence is contagious.
That it encourages confession
which is really a transfer of power.
Beauty can make us so stupid
and you can't even look at me in the face.

At night, I recite prayers
into your soft, bleached hair.
Turning away, you remind me
of that Venus painting
from Velásquez,
same neck, except yours
is more punk. More west coast.
Maybe too much hard living too young.
I think of all the women
turned away from us in art.
We see only the slopes
of shoulders and spine,
an arched hip, each patch of body
in elongated slumber,
a balmy and unsullied sleep.
Your ribs heave like tendrils
when you inhale the moony night
which is really day now,
the seasons all fucked up
and reversed by your body.

THE THURSDAY OF TWO BODIES

a man
prostrate
head down
black steps subway
platform at the top
of the stairs
gurgling
or coughing
or choking
or clearing his throat
fallen
the sounds fighting
in his mouth
bird-like
so jurassic
only one person
approaches
it is too early
to overdose
west 4th
the A and the C
arrive
simultaneously
take the A it skips
23rd to port
authority catch the bus

to work
grade
on the highway
route 78
the bus slows
jersey: on the right—
three trucks
and a car stopped
each
more suspect
than the next
a man standing
hands cover his mouth
like chapel doors
agape
another man
lying
prostrate
face down
on the asphalt
symphony of limbs
some blood
but not like the movies
black marks
not quite bruises
god
there is no

respectful way
to say this but
it is
important
this same body
kept multiplying
not fetal but laid out
dissected
as if hallucinating as if
i were mad someone
was cupping
his face another
woman looked on
i am teaching
judith butler today
i arrive
to class as if
i had not seen
bodies i open a
powerpoint
i call
on ryan first
a nice kid
from jersey
most thursdays
are not
like this

ALICE AND EILEEN

Alice is all over *Chelsea Girls*, and it takes me back
to that interview I did in Paris when I was so sloppy
and just twenty-four and Alice, with those big eyebrows
and black blazer, utterly shy and yet demanding, asked me flat
out if I was a poet and I didn't have the nerve. We both cried
about her brother in 1988 and her illness and Ted
and she told me about how Creeley would talk himself backwards
into a poem, and she sang a Korean folk song
and here is Alice Notley singing aloud in the ninth arrondissement
and here is me, too startled to check my notes and flash forward
six years to my apartment in Lisbon and Eileen
is hanging out a large window looking over the pigeon stones
and I barely have the gall to mingle in the same square foot
while she eats a sandwich and drinks Perrier and I just
remember how *Chelsea Girls* was really about the small
victories of hunger, and how she jumped up and down in anger
like a child while trying to sell a teevee for a measly ten bucks
and now here she is in Lisbon with thick bread and me, throwing
back some port wine waiting for the nineteen-year-old girl named
Tereshina I met at a tiny bar in the shape of a chapel
with its sweaty blue tiles who agreed to come
to an American's apartment in Príncipe Real and sing fado
and here is Eileen in Lisbon and there was Alice in Paris, France.

When you are to read for Eileen at St. Mark's, you take her big book
of narrow, spiraling poems from start to finish and put one hand
on the belly of a pregnant friend and ask the unborn
to make the decision by kicking. The baby is silent
for the first twenty pages which is a shame because those are some
of your favorites, but we find one called Road Warrior, maybe too short,
and something about cumming, coming home, and wait for her,
wait for me, and the cadence makes you think get up, lana turner,
and here are all the things you can learn from girls, from women.
Sometimes you dream about that night in Lisbon where
people flooded the stairwell and Alexei read in her green jumpsuit,
that one that only she could pull off even though around her eyes,
you could see lovers gone wrong. People listened to Tereshina
sing fado in the front room and the sound carried out
into the streets, all the way to the park you find out the next day,
and there was Eileen in the big floral armchair and somewhere
in the room was your cousin, your student, a tall man you loved,
and the quiet, chilling orbit of the whole room slowly aging.

TELL ME WHAT YOU KNOW ABOUT DISMEMBERMENT
—after Bhanu Kapil

We can live without limbs

                                    unless

they are our siblings.

RHODE ISLAND WEDDING

After Kai's wedding, he hit his head skinny-dipping
on the cement by the pool, ended up in the ER while his bride slept,
her father an inappropriate Gemini questioning me all night long,
sober like a righteous lion. I wore a long dress and you and I
got in a bad fight. I sat in mud under a short shrub of a tree
and watched others stumble through the farm
where the wedding was held, where the tent sprang into life
like a heaven in the middle of an empty cosmos. My dress was wrecked.
I had bought it in Lisbon and the woman had told me how pretty I looked,
big gown, hips with a slit right up the front, cupped breasts, a sash wrapped
under the bust line. The shop was in a basement. She told me her father
was born in Africa just like mine. I believed her. I said, *yes, I look pretty.*
And she said *yes, you look pretty.* And I was in a basement feeling so pretty
and now in a black field of anonymous weeds in Rhode Island,
sulking under a tree, not so drunk, but thinking I looked
(with the summer insects cozying up to my ankles) like a beautiful fool,
something out of a novel where all women are posed this way—
untouchable until proven unruly, ugly. I counted my toes.
I counted my toes and ruined that dress and remembered how I took
    two boats
to get here, to this tree shelter, to these conclusions.
As a child, I would invent mothers that were nothing like my own.
They would wear long yellow nightgowns like traveling sunlights,
big angular hats, pale, pale skin—they'd be so star-like
that they could never survive even my imagination, bursting into vapors.
They would say to me in my white petticoat: *you look so pretty*

91

and I'd believe them. Because I am so gullible when covered,
putting on airs, pretending myself a goddess or queen, in reality,
a vain slob at the foot of a tree that can barely keep its spine,
hiding poorly, counting my toes, the muddy ten.

WHILE I KEEP MAKING THE ROOM BRIGHTER

in skerries, ireland,

you are across the shore

                                           i am wearing a fairy dress

                wreath of white baby's breath

                      in my hair

you have a beard and

                look so irish   i so indian

                      we get a cheap hotel
     a bathtub

            and a bus   that runs through
the countryside

                    i feel faint around you
                    like an image that keeps
             clipping

                              in an ancient projector
            what if i die

tomorrow, riding my bike

                                              through the grassy streets
of montauk

don't be heartbroken. i loved you even when

        how do things become   what is the mass of

                              not like on vacation when we're
            mostly drunk

            but like when we run baths and peel fruit

and curl against each other

            like when you told me, after nine years of being
together,

                        that you saw the tower fall
        (the second one, of course)

                                              in person.

nine years.

how did i not know this.   what does it mean.

　　that there is no room for you where there is me

that i take up

　　　　all the air? that you don't mind?

　　so you have to live   with

　　　　while i keep making the room brighter

you search for that inch

　　　　　　　　　　　of shadow

　　　　in which to conceal the silhouettes

　　　of men

or nightmares or

　　　do you have nightmares? is this a poem?

IN THE BEGINNING

There is Muddy Waters in the floods with Bach,
Sarah Vaughan and Verdi on a float. There is a small utopia
in the form of a raft, bobbing down a small canal in the left
hemisphere of a brain. There is a canal in Berlin.
There is a heart and heartbreak busting new geographies,
making a novel planet of all of us and a portraitist
painting commissions of the wealthy Quebecois
in a Montreal loft, the snows in soft collision
with the community gardens outside, sterile
like the smiles of the family with their severe warmth.
Oil paintings take years to dry and I want a longevity
built on chemical tears of water, potassium,
a pleasuring glucose making a home in the nerves
of your face. Infants cannot weep. Your infant is the first
executioner whom you kiss. Openly. Whom you bathe like
a clock impersonating your adulthood, like a pile of dead asters
interrogating you from the window. Asta is the name
of a dog from an old detective serial called *The Thin Man*
where Nick and Nora drank endless martinis and flirted with guns.
There are guns in the snowbank and in the classroom,
in the casinos and someone's car, in the fire safe of a wealthy man.
When men rage, they want to take everyone with them.
We mistake vigils for vigilantes. Sometimes I throw
so many clothes around my room—
piles of silk coats and tulle skirts. They begin to take the shape
of people. I wake up in the night and they look like

flat bodies evacuated out of the fabric,
an army of ballerinas gone missing.

CHURCH GIRLS

I go for hymns and the Ave Maria.
I can't resist the white blur

of choir capes or copper
pipes making the crucifix

shudder. Jesus is shuddering
up there, looking out at

the central aisle
of his church, tubular

like the fuselage
of an airplane.

I sing along. I stay

because years of Catholic school
have stapled me to wooden benches

by the gravitas of nuns.

But I am a good sinner.
Yes. There is a club

where we mourn
the angels

and the way the sky dopes

in November, gray and chill.
We aren't afraid anymore.

Not of sacrilege nor the carcass
building the country.

In church, there are no nations
just bloodshed.

I admit that Gabriel
was always my favorite.

His first appearance, a vision of terror.
And poor Daniel, his receiver

bedridden for days.

SALMONFLY

I play the piano to feel all the keys together, hugging. The sacrificed bird, the Siberian girl, the planet ripe with salmonflies, sowing the earth into a drink. There is Ovid at his Roman sex party; there is SalmonFly traveling back into time, the centripetal guru, telling the Latin poet to not kiss his mistress on the neck. Now, he's in Frankfurt, hiding his small eggs in the aluminum kitchens, whizzing across the roofs of mouths. Children adore him. Even a sponge cocktail, a huckleberry bush, the heavens for SalmonFly who loves water and thorns, who does not eat in adult life, who plays dead when the piano stops, when the girl at the black voluptuous instrument shifts from Mendelssohn to Bach.

IN CALIFORNIA, EVERYTHING ALREADY LOOKS LIKE AN AFTERLIFE

Before he is sick, he surfs the Pacific.
After he is sick, his faint body is pulled
from the water just in time to know
something is expanding. Leia goes over.
Just as friends, she says.
She sleeps in his bed, makes coffee,
tackles the wild zinnias of the Santa Barbara
hills, bends the flora to her spells.
The brain controls everything
except his nearly lifeless foot
moving to a Steely Dan cover.

All his orchids are crooked in the greenhouse
and the cats are missing. *Too many coyotes*,
he once said. When he was well,
everything survived. The orchids grew
erect, the coyotes were spineless, and Leia
stitched things together on her porch
exactly half a mile from the ocean.

Does anyone ever die in California,
I wonder. Leia enshrines him with eucalyptus
and Neruda, calls us, sleeps fetal now in LA.
You want to hear a love story, someone says.
Meaning them. Meaning this thing,
not quite knowable to us, her hand

on his laughing foot, the only part still alive,
it seems, the contract of their intimacy
that is not quite love, not quite
anything we've seen or can name.

EMPLOYEES ONLY

I open your mouth at a booth.

On the table: glasses slick
with shrinking ice

a lick
of whiskey film

gluing them together.

We are surrounded.
But I don't care.

I don't care.
I don't care.

You see, there has been
a week of rain

and so much sadness.

And here,
we are an ark.

HOW TO HAVE A BABY IN THE ANTHROPOCENE

Do it with someone who gets fresh water
not a city kid, but an outlaw
who can diagnose an egg, scale a wall
in the Adirondacks. Have the baby
and survive it. Learn to live
with constant foreshadowing, days dizzy
with anticipation. Befriend the desert
and forest bats and even those eels,
flooding the parking lots,
spun around trees above silver cars.
A dead eel with its dead eyes looks just
as stirring above water, thread into a tree line.
Have the baby, defer the end.
Get a pediatrician
with a specialty in trapping time,
who can replace a kneecap with sugar
red and full of a synthetic love.
Have a smart kid. Play him Bowie.
Tell him about the '80s. Tell him about decades
of men, decadent men. Wrap your kid
in a blanket and float him down the Nile
and if it dries out, the Euphrates.
Might as well make it biblical—
as biblical as the sky on the run.
Birth a fugitive. Let him drift
under highways, listen

to conspiracies about salmon
with gold-flaked eyes,
fictions of the sea.
Let him remember your belly's
lullabies of hell, still a sweet thought
about a birthday
when birthdays were not days of blame.
Tell him about cities
and how you lived there, once.
And something called an intersection
where you slipped your hand into
someone else's on Boulevard Villette
and gazed towards a skyline of soot,
mistaking it for a future.
Don't be melodramatic.
It is the worst kind of defeat.
It is the opposite of parenthood.
Be a parent, for god's sake.
Tell him about the earth
and more lovingly, its tumbling
civilizations, rolling over
one another, gathering
and gathering,
gathering into his exact
hallowed form.

NO BLACK. NO ASIAN. NO FEMME.

On east 13th, we eat Filipino food
and talk virtual worlds of desire.

People don't want contradictions
when they fuck, Phillip says.

They want the world affirmed.

She shows me the phone.
Those words burst, bloom in headless
profiles of abs and pelvic bones:

No Black. No Asian. No Femme.
No Black. No Asian. No Femme.
No Black. No Asian. No Femme.

A rose is a rose is a rose.
We order another glass of champagne
or maybe it was a sidecar.

I cry a little into a banana leaf.
I don't know why this stuff still kills me
to be a couple of brown femmes spitting
with laughter at their own repulsion
projected flagrantly on the white screen.

What does it mean to be undesirable.
An answer the internet cannot give.

Dear Phillip, I do not know.
Dear Phillip, each of your utterances
is a plow through my weary, weary heart.
Dear Phillip, what was that thing
we mistook for a liberation.

WHITE INSOMNIA

I am having the dream again
where my mother is a broom.

Check on your sister, the broom says.

She is sleeping on a bed made of lava-rock ruin,
wrapped in sweet-pea vines,

the aerial rootlets climbing clockwise,
posing in their leafstalk, a hand-stitched

quilt covers her from a rain that brings
seawater to her flounder sleep.

There are many insects here.
Softly, in a corner,

Satie is playing.
I often dream in melodies.

I watch the sleeping girl
through a few shrugged pillars, witness

orange monarchs sweeping close to her eyes.

I sweep.
I am sweeping monarchs with my mother.

Unconscious women, even in dreams,
make me fearful.

One day my sister will die,
which had never occurred to me—

and still seems, in the bedrock of dream,
impossible.

BAUDELAIRE SAYS: WRITE A POEM TO YOUR CREDITORS

The rattling battery. The human face. The adventure of sleep
that we enter every night, the cynical way we evade dreaming.
How voluptuous humiliation can feel, how reckless we are with talent.
The violent, erotic energy of a cathedral. The hum of chapels, abandoned.
The small rains. The togetherness of leaves. Dead, purple carnations.
Debt. A thousand dollars owed to a hospital in Providence. The ER.
The breathing tube and bag of electrolytes. That nurse. Girlish.
How some of us laugh while hunted. The smooth genitalia of WASPs.
The way we bet. What we gamble with. Our fungal hearts. Our heart.
Our way out of poems. Our soldiers. Mali. The bureaucracy of kills.
The belief in light. Cults. Chandeliers like Madonnas. What we owe.

ACKNOWLEDGMENTS

Poems in this book have appeared in the following journals and magazines:

Academy of American Poets Poem-a-Day, "The Jungle"

The Adroit Journal, "Conversion," "Fabric in Tribeca," and "Venus, Aged"

Bennington Review, "Amsterdam"

BOAAT, "At the Public Library, Surrounded by the Unlikely in Montauk, NY"

Chicago Review, "In the Beginning" and "No Black. No Asian. No Femme."

Columbia Poetry Review, "Coloring Hour" and "Running in the Suburbs"

The Common, "Good Boys"

The Common Poetry Feature Online, "White People Always Want to Tell Me That They Grew Up Poor"

Court Green, "Coloring Hour" and "The Poet Holds a Gun"

CURA magazine, "In Which I Become a Mythology and Also, Executed" and "Modern Nation-States"

Denver Quarterly, "Alice and Eileen"

Hayden's Ferry Review, "Bad Habit"

The Margins, "Belleville" and "Night, the First"

The Missouri Review Poem of the Week, "Sonora"

The New Yorker, "Scylla and Charybdis"

PANK, "Dior" and "Indigo"

Ploughshares, "Rhode Island Wedding"

Rattle (Poets Respond), "Nukemap.com" and "Why We Drink"

THRUSH Poetry Journal, "Regret Is a Blue Dive"

Tin House, "The Eulogy" and "In California, Everything Already Looks like an Afterlife"

Two Peach, "Five of Swords"

The Volta, "SalmonFly"

The Walrus, "Manchester to Lisbon"

I feel extraordinarily lucky to have a large, unruly, and generous group of friends without whom this book would not be possible. These people have nourished me through their own art, brilliance, humor, and they are my family: Elisa Giardina Papa, Kevin Kemble, Judith Benchimol, Joey Chriqui, Saad Khan, Mimi Cabell, Kai Franz, Ryan Poe, Derek Woods, Rivkah Gevinson, Jeff Scheible, Rachelle Conley, Catherine Pond, Dan Kraines, June Rockefeller, Alex Dimitrov, Anna Vargo, Camille Pouliot, Sarah Morris, Brent Utter, Randi Gill-Sadler, Catherine Tice, Sarah Riggs and Omar Berrada, Amanda Phillips, Megan Garr, Anna Arov, Lindsay Thomas, Eng-Beng Lim, Fabri Giardina Papa, Christie Ann Reynolds, Jessica Carr, Mario Sanchez, Owen McLeod, Mikael Awake, Cara Blue Adams, Adam Peterson, Lauren Clark, Victoria Redel, Jennifer Gilmore, Adam Markovic, Sharon Okun, Marc Steinberg, Natasha Hakimi, Bükem Reitmeyer, Asher Faerstein, Danielle and Andre Aguiar, Bishnupriya Ghosh, and Stephanie LeMenager. A special, emphasized thank you to Kaveh Akbar, Lisa Hiton, and Lee Norton, who took the time to read the manuscript.

I would like to thank my colleagues and friends in the Department of English at Lafayette College for their support, especially Lee Upton and Alix Ohlin, two of the kindest and most well-read people I've ever met. I have loved trying to keep up with your brains and equally enjoyed failing to do so.

I never fail to think that without meeting Sarah Riggs and Sharifa Rhodes-Pitts in Paris at the age of twenty-four, I may not have become a writer. That was a life-changing workshop. Thank you. And of course, thank you to the Paris writers who challenged me during a critical time in my poetic development: Helen O'Keefe, Bruce Sherfield, Alberto Rigitenni, Chris Newens, Albert Alla, Isabel Harding, Peter Brown, Ida Lødemel Tvedt, Malik Crumpler, and Jason Francis McGimsey. Thank you to Penelope Fletcher at The Red Wheelbarrow Bookstore and Phyllis Cohen at Berkeley Books of Paris for the warm, engaging, and radical way that you have supported the literary misfits of that city.

Thank you to the Edward F. Albee Foundation and the Swatch Art Peace Hotel artist residency for your support and fellowships.

Equally important, thank you to the staff at Joseph Leonard and the Marlton in New York City.

A number of writerly friendships and mentorships have developed over the past few years. I would not be the writer I am without the following people: Kevin Young, Kaveh Akbar, sam sax, Hannah Lillith Assadi, Taylor Johnson, Peg and Bob Boyers, Rosanna Warren, Dan Chiasson, Robert Pinsky, Kazim Ali, Bernie Kaplan, Damian Rogers, and Vincent Small.

Matthew Dickman, editor extraordinaire, this book has benefited so much from your imagination and critique. Thank you to Tony Perez, Jakob Vala, and the entire team at Tin House for your support and creative energy in making this book possible.

Mom and Dad, every single day I pray that you will both live forever. I am adrift without your voices and love.

Josh, thank you for letting me become the most complicated version of myself over the past years. Not many partnerships are based on that extraordinary kind of love and acceptance and I feel lucky that we have built a life on laughter, planning big and elaborate dinners with our friends, and encouraging each other's endless intellectual and emotional curiosities. Thank you for leaving me alone when I needed it and for giving me a hug when I needed it and for showing me how people can be fully dimensional and still worthy of love. I love your mind and how you make lentils. I love that you read three different newspapers by the time I wake up in the morning. I love that you always carry the keys so I don't have to and are willing to close all the cupboards in the house after I've thoughtlessly kept them open for reasons that mystify both of us. I love our friendship. You are an unbelievable person and I should tell you this more often. This is so personal that I know it is making you cringe. I deeply enjoy making you cringe.

This book is dedicated to my older sisters who are remarkable people. You never let me get away with unkindness. You call me out when I'm being a snot. You have loved me with such unconditional ferocity, I find it startling over and over again.